Justice
Verses
Life

A book of short storied poems based on elements of my personal and professional life.

BEVERLEY CAMPBELL

© 2022 Beverley Campbell
www.justiceverseslife.com

ISBN 978-1-8381190-3-4

A Spirit First Creatives publication from
Black Stone Press & DMC Books

Distributed By
Black Stone Press & DMC Books
27 Trory Street, Norwich, UK
office@dmcconsultancy.co.uk

Design by Nadia Deen
www.deenwebsitedesign.com

To my darling daughter Samantha,
who as a child inspired me to achieve
and as a glorious adult has
supported me in every new dream I
have attempted to make a reality.

CONTENTS

ABOUT JUSTICE

For many years my close friends have referred to me as "Justice" which partly refers to my profession as a family law solicitor but more often to my constant need to ensure that those around me are treated fairly and with consideration, regardless of the situation. However, don't get it twisted, I am fierce about ensuring that liberties are not taken.

Over the past three decades I have enjoyed using my love of the written word to create a series of short stories, written as poetry that depict elements of life that I have witnessed personally and professionally and what those incidents have taught me. I have had the pleasure of performing my work for many years in different venues and settings and although I enjoy the physical interaction and often riotous laughter received from the audience, I am mostly impressed by how many of them have expressed how my body of work has resonated with them personally. That to me, means everything.

I have never sought to judge, dictate or believe that I am always right. But by striving to be a conscious woman I have learned that as humans, we are all different, and there is nothing wrong with that. All any one of us can do is, find what works for us and do the best you can.

I really hope you enjoy my first publication and through your support and encouragement, it will not be my last.

"BWOY, MI REMEMBER AH SELFRIDGES, RIVER ISLAND AND JD SPORTS WE USED TO GO,

BORIS MEK THE PEOPLE LOCK THEM SHOP, LIKE THE MAN FROM DELMONTI, HIM SAID "NO".

MY YOUNGER YEARS AND WHAT I LEARNT

Section One

SISTERS, PLEASE WEAR YOUR SIZE

Sisters we really need to wear our size
We all know that our bodies we really can't
disguise

I learned this painful lesson way back in time
Never thought my shame would be put into rhyme

Hot day in 1977 Tulse hill boys were coming down
All week the jungle telegraph spread the news
around.

Being bigger at school could sometimes be really
hard
Some thought they were better than you because
you were large

So, I did my hair, new cherry lip gloss went on
Next was my new pinstripe shirt, wanted to look
like a female Don

Bought from my granny's Janet Frazer catalogue, I
was sure it would fit me.
But as I huffed and puffed there seemed to be a
cruel conspiracy.

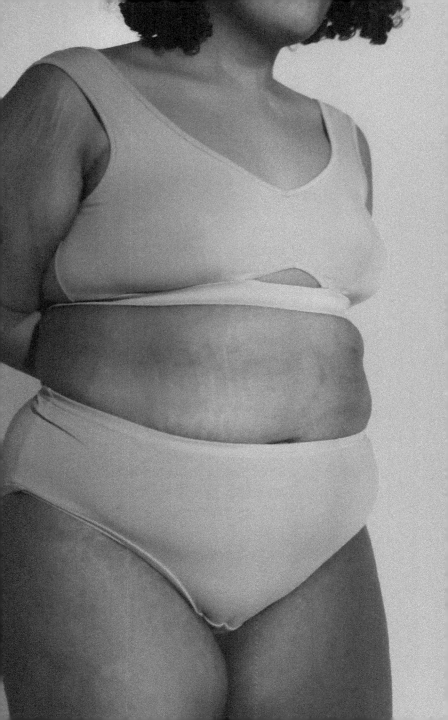

It did not work, when at last the buttons did up
My breasts looked like large crushed saucers
rather than shapely cups

I decided that this fancy shirt had to wear
I had to impress, I had new shoes, new shirt, slick
hair

So, with the imagination that has made me the
woman I am today
I set about creating an illusion in some way.

I unpicked the sides, oh the shirt started to feel
loose
But across the chest still felt as tight as a noose

So, I unpicked the back, letting air and skin roll
free
Now from the front at least, this shirt looked as if it
fit me.

I then put on my cardigan to cover up my crime
No one needed to know my shirt had no sides or
behind

Admiring glances from friends I later met in the
street
Meant I could try to forget the new shoes were
burning my feet

Finally sitting in assembly that morning

I thought I only had to stop myself from yawning

Until Ms Ottey called out, it was too warm, we
would smell
Said we had to take our cardigans off, oh God I'm
in hell

People reacted slowly but I could only pray
This woman wasn't going to back down, not her,
no way.

Everyone obeyed, I could not. My shirt was not in
one piece
I looked all around, still praying for some release

I stared straight ahead, indigent to the end
I really knew then how it felt to sweat like a pig my
friend

She saw me and demanded I should report to the
head
Why, oh why had I not stayed at home in my bed?

The head was quite amazed to see a "goody
goody" like me
I told her I was being victimised for being fat by
Ms Ottey

Said she had inferred fat people smelled and I was
upset
Pretended to cry, making sure our eyes never met.

You see the Head carried a few too many pounds like me
So, I played on that to gain some sympathy

She said detention would be a suitable punishment for me
I couldn't care less as long as my belly no one got to see

After that detention I forgot about looking for a man
In my mind I had only one plan.

I got rid of that shirt, didn't care how much I had to pay.
What if she had forced me to take off my cardigan that day?

I would have had to fight her, just to save myself from shame
Hit a teacher living in my granny's house, you wouldn't walk again.

So, from that very painful day to this.
I have learnt that it ain't mine if it doesn't fit.

So, ladies please remember, not all of us can be slim
Cream cakes and chocolate could be your passion rather than the gym

But please check yourself and consider this.
You must look better, no matter what you wear, if it
actually fits.

———

OPP
(OTHER PEOPLE'S PROPERTY)

Always said that she could never do it, wasn't
down with that plan
But then she met that particular man

Said he never lied to her, saying he was stressed at
home
He came direct, said he just wanted her, needed
them to be alone

At first, she resisted, not willing to go down that
road
Couldn't consider sleeping with someone's else's
man in her abode

But every time she saw him her body began to
sweat
She had never been so nervous with any other
man she'd met

Her heart pounded until she could hear it in her
ears
She constantly dreamt of being with him, just
ignoring her fears

She could never tell anyone what she desperately
wanted to do
And lied when friends asked if she'd met someone
new

He was constantly on her mind throughout the
night and day
She could not push his mental image away

So, she decided to do it, and took up with OPP
Joined the ranks of those women she'd scorned
and said she'd never be.

Months went by, they were in a blur of pure
romance
Although circumstances meant no restaurants or
even attending a local dance

But before long they were seen, but were so
caught up in their affair
They never noticed his woman, her best friend,
was even standing there.

His woman wanted to scream, to cuss and carry on
bad
Her mind was racing, she thought she would go
mad

Then reality kicked in, you reap what you sow, so
she had nothing to say

After all, she didn't two years ago when his last
woman caught her that way.

I'm not moralising but here's some advice that
comes completely free
Anything a brother would do to her; he'd do to
you or me.

———————————

THAT MAN

Years ago, I had a friend who always looked out for
me
I really thought a better man there could never be

He was good looking, respectful and kind
Always available for me, saying I was always on his
mind

We decided that we should be lovers rather than
just friends
But unfortunately, I fear, that was the beginning of
the end.

At the beginning we had so much fun, it was pure
joy
And the loving, well let me say, he was a serious
kinda boy

But after a while the dates went from frequent to
just a few
He was never around; I didn't know what to do

Now he seemed to only have time for his
anonymous friends
When it came to me, his Nokia battery had always
come to an end.

Christmas 1985 was just round the corner, and I was so brock
When I got a wicked tax rebate, I couldn't believe my luck

Thought of the bills I could pay to take the pressure off my head
And the gifts I could buy for my child, even a new bed

I never realised the man was there watching when the cheque came
Suddenly, I had a best friend and lover all over again

Later in the car he said he'd seen a "gold chops" he wanted to buy
A bargain at £300 – I swear I tell no lie.
Said he left the jeweller a deposit of £30.00
Said his girl would soon come and bring the rest around.

I said "so you have gal that have that kinda money to waste on you?
Because I know that foolishness I would never do.

Him draw brake, seh me too fastie, him nah put up with that kinda thing

Him jump out and slam the car door so hard, me poor ears start to ring.

Now you may think I'd be stranded, those who
don't know me
Because even though he loved to drive, I owned
that car key

I just moved over, adjusted my controls
And drove off past the fool, fool boy as he stood
out in the cold

Later he came over, man still ah huff and a blow
Ready for argument now, look like something out
of a comedy show

I must honest, his language I have had to change
Decent people like you would not appreciate his
full range.

He said "you see you, you is not a bad looking girl
Your big but you look good enough to make your
way in the world

But the reason you can't keep a man is you too
mean you see
Every day I borrow your car, the petrol needle deh
pan "E"

You work in a big office and every Friday you get
pay
You would never consider pushing a little £50 my
way

I like to smoke me tings and you know me brock,
even though me a try
You would never go out and buy something and
bring in for the I"

The boy started walking up and down as if he was
policing my place
Cussing and carrying on bad, in my house, a me
him cum to trace

"You supposed to fry sprats on a Friday like my
mother used to do
Give me a set of car keys, I shouldn't need to keep
ah beg you."

I asked "what happens when I need to drive to
school or to my job?
The man said "simple gal, tek cab"

"You can't walk go a bus stop, something wrong
with you?
Before you could afford car, you never use to wait
for the number 2?"

I had to look at this boy and consider how him so
bright
I was going to tell him how many blue beads mek
five that night

But I never bother because I learned a lesson from
my former friend

When he disrespected me, our affair had to come to an end.

I know if I did parn something and lick him one of we going to dead
So, I bid him a fond farewell, kiss my teeth and went straight to my bed

In life you'll always find people who will try to take liberty
Learn who they are before you give away yourself, much less your car key.

"LORD, YOU KNOW ME, I CAN'T SURVIVE ON PRISON FOOD,

BUT IF HE DECIDE TO LICK ME, BELIEVE I AM GOING TO GET VERY RUDE."

WHEN I FELT THAT I WAS A BIG WOMAN, BUT STILL HAD LESSONS TO LEARN

Section Two

SOMEBODY ALMOST RAN OFF WITH MY STUFF

All my stuff was flung into a dirty bag and hauled
along the floor
Dragged along like rubbish being taken out of my
open door

My full brown eyes that witnessed both joy and
sorrow
My chapped hands which had supported me
without the need to borrow

My strong black thighs which carried me through
this journey of life.
My bare fingers signifying my inability to be
chosen as someone's wife.

Somebody almost ran off with all my stuff.

My fleshy bosoms where favoured ones had the
pleasure to lay
Before vacating my loving arms with promises of
returning one day.

Without my permission, consent, or warning that
you were going to leave
My heart and soul were being taken away, leaving
my carcass on its knees

I wanted to shout out," you can't take what does
not belong to you."
But I did not think I would be heard, couldn't think
of what to do.

I needed to demand that I was given back my stuff
immediately
To scream out "you can't have my stuff, it only
belongs to me."

I had to reclaim all the characteristics that made
me, me.
Yet I watched as they were thrown around,
obtained completely free.

No demon spirit had run off with my stuff, just a
plain simple man
Wondering through life with only an ego but no
sustainable plan.

So careless with his own existence yet I gave him
dominion over my life.
Saw me as a series of one-night stands whilst I saw
myself as his future wife.

He was going without acknowledging my loss or

my right to grieve
Did not even consider my existence when he got
up to leave?

What was the reason I could not call out "thief"
and demand an enquiry?
Was it because I had in fact given away my stuff, all
of me?

In a desperate attempt to have someone say he
would always stay
I was willing to trade all I had, which meant I gave
myself away.

Suddenly I found my voice, started shouting for all
I was worth
"You give me back my stuff, it is mine, all I possess
on this earth".

Do you know, the worst thing was he didn't even
know what he had?
My stuff was so insignificant he had just flung the
good in with the bad.

He had thrown my precious stuff in with all his
other mess
Did not see, consider, or recognise that they were
all I had left.

This could have been, to me at least, the biggest
robbery of all time.

But as he never valued me, using, and disposing of my treasure was just fine.

Someone almost got away with all my stuff, nearly got away with me.
Please treasure and protect your stuff as it is all you'll ever have or can ever be.

———————————

LOVE IN THE AISLES

Bright and early food shopping was all I had on my mind
Did it first thing as no long queues I didn't want to find.

Concentrating strictly on the freshness of the fruit
Noticed a brother checking me out, he did look kinda cute

As I walked past, I heard, "woman what a way you sweet"
I had to look at him straight from his head to his feet

I smiled as the brother looked extremely fine
Thought he'd get on his with shopping whilst I got on with mine

But he followed me saying "boy you only buy the best"
I had to respond with "Why would I consider anything less?"

Wondered why he had no trolley, wasn't carrying anything in his hand

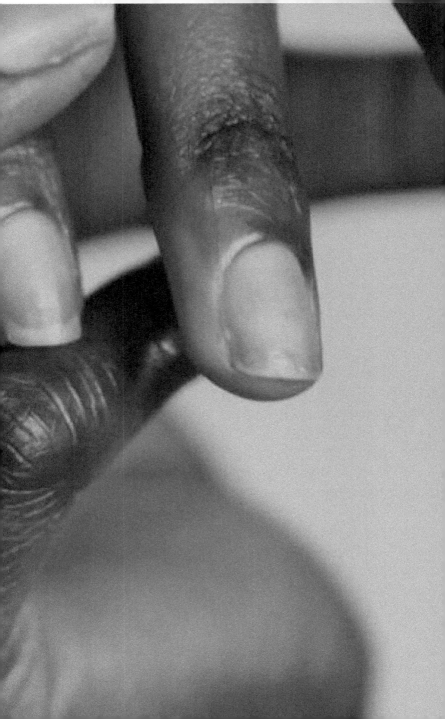

However, I also checked, there was no wedding band

Later I saw him talking to a little boy
They looked so sweet together as they chose a toy

From then on he kept appearing then disappearing into thin air
Said he needed my details as we were made to be a pair

I laughed and walked away to join the checkout line
Looked around to say goodbye but there was no sign

Then I spied him, with a woman, it looked like the boy was their son
A beautiful family unit, just doing their own thing and having fun.

Now, I was not jealous, the man was never mine
Plus, I now suspected he might be pretty, but he was not that fine

I decided to forget the incident as they were leaving the store
Without a backward glance he went straight out of the door.

Then I heard "I need your number, have to see you

again"
I said I thought he was with his son and his
girlfriend.

No, baby, don't worry, that was my sister and her
son
Sweetheart, nuff man ah player, but I am not one

So, I said, "she is your sister, oh that is cool.
Call her back, she looks like a girl I used to know
from school"

He kissed his teeth. I was just too damn bright he
said
And without another word, my man simply turned
his head.

He moved out of that supermarket at a hasty pace.
No longer talking about wanting to come over to
my place.

Driving past the bus stop I saw the family
sheltering from the rain
Decided to teach him that women may look
normal but can also be insane

I called out "excuse me" he nearly jumped out of
his skin
She came over while he looked like a stroke was
going to kill him.

I only asked her for directions, and she kindly gave
me just that
Whilst he stood behind her looking like a
frightened, cornered little rat.

So early in the morning the brother's plan was to
disrespect me and his girl
Is this how little he thinks of the women in this
world?

Thank God maturity has changed me in some way
I woulda cuss him and fling some tins in his head,
back in the day.

But I'm too decent, never been held down by
Tesco's security yet
But don't test me or you may find out how crazy a
disrespected sista can get.

PARDON ME, WHAT DID YOU SAY?

I have always prided myself on living a dignified,
decent life
Felt it was beneath me to get involved in
arguments and strife.

So, you can imagine my disgust late one-night last
week
When my phone rang and I heard a loud, animal
like shriek

"Leave my man alone" she screamed "he belongs
to me not you!"
"Hold on", I said, "who the hell do you think your
talking to?"

She kept on shouting I had no right to be sleeping
with her lover.
I couldn't believe my man was deceiving me with
another.

Said they'd been together for six months; it was
the real thing.
He had said she was the only one who he wanted
to wear his ring.

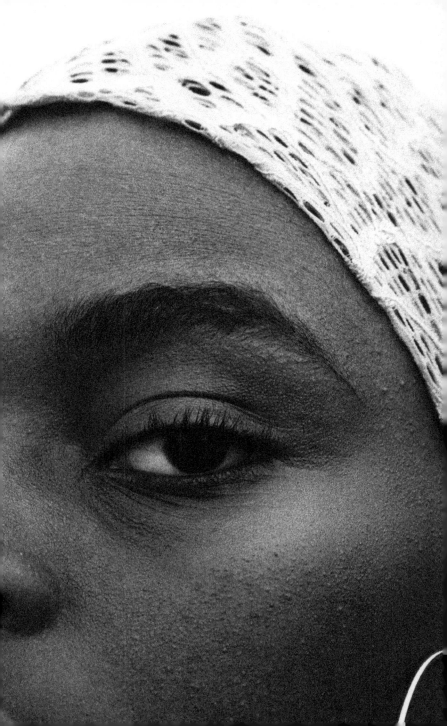

What, I'd been with this man for years and yet to
this date
He'd never mentioned marriage, well now it was
too damn late.

I tried to talk to her as an intelligent, strong black
female
However, her swearing and shouting just
continued off the scale.

Despite my distress I still tried to reason with this
withheld call.
Insisting that we should not be involved in a verbal
brawl

Said he was the proper recipient of her and now,
my anger
Told her to ring and challenge him on his mobile
number

We needed to tell him his deceit had given us trust
issues
This had to stop, we would no longer allow our
hearts to be abused

Her response was to threaten me with grievous
bodily harm
Planned to acid me in the street, I heard with some
alarm

Forget being decent now, I'm vex, and madness

came over me.
Nobody is going to ring and threaten me because
their mobile calls are free

I told that gal, you really want me to take off your
head
Don't make me have to forget myself or somebody
going to dead

Make sure you don't pass your place and call my
damn phone again.
And don't you worry, me done, you can have the
lied man.

Said she'd call whenever she liked if I kept
sleeping with her Len.
I beg your pardon, I said, call that name again.

Beg you tell me girl, who the hell is Len?
There was a moment's silence and then...

"Sorry mam, wrong number" and with that the call
ended with a click
And from that day to this I never heard again from
that chick.

The front door opened, and my man came walking
in.
Up to now I don't confess how close his
belongings came to my dustbin.

HOW THE HELL AM I GOING TO MANAGE?

Oh, my Lord, they mugged me, got away with nearly all my wages
You know how long I worked to earn that money, it took me ages

How am I going to pay all those bills that have just come in?
I don't even have the choice of whether to sink or swim

There's no food in the cupboards, no meat in my fridge
I don't know how the hell we are going to live.

Some may think cutting back on food would be a good step for me
But what about the rent, gas, and the electricity?

I know that when you buy one at Iceland, you can get one for free
But unless they are giving away everything, they can't even save me

Why are things so hard, life just seems so bad
No matter how I try, stress and pressure just drives
me mad

If they had tried to grab my bag from me in the
street
I could make sure their maker they would get to
meet

But they don't rob you to your face, its national
insurance and taxation
That is what they use to rob the nation.

I work from early morning until late at night
But when I calculate my wages, that figure never
sees daylight

The deductions on my wage slip are always more
than I believe
How are we supposed to live on the little this
government leaves?

ALL YOU NEED IS LOVE

They met so casually
Yet they fell so intensively

She was his Nubian Queen, and he was her Ebony
King
He supported her dreams and she inspired him to
achieve everything

Over the years they became professional man and
wife
Worked hard to obtain all the ingredients for a
successful life.

After two children he remained totally faithful to
his significant other
And she was still a down to earth sister who just
loved the brother

But stress and pressure caused arguments
between husband and wife
Somehow, he lost sight of the important things in
life

When the arguments started, he said he'd had
more than enough

Articulating and compromising right then was just
too tough

It was only a slap, it was never really meant
Just something he did to put an end to their
argument

Offered to go to Relate, wanted her to forgive and
forget
Gave her diamond earrings but their eyes never
met

She was confused, distressed, too ashamed to talk
Thinking how she had said if that ever happened
to her, she'd walk

Six months later a push, a slap, a punch in the side
This time he felt his actions were justified

It was her fault; she knew that he was suffering
from stress
Why could she not just shut up, she had caused all
this mess

How did she expect them to move on?
When she just insisted on carrying the arguments
on?

Countless incidents of makeup covering up their
latest disagreement

She'd be angry, plan to leave but would later relent

It came to an end on a Sunday morning, after a party the night before
He grabbed her by the throat as she ran for the door

He was so convinced everyone last night was avoiding his eyes
When he accused her of telling them her face showed no surprise

This time she didn't remain passive, would not give him control
She now refused to adopt her previous downtrodden role

She called him a weak, wife beater and said that she was leaving him
He said without her he would feel as if he had lost a limb

He cursed, then begged, promised he would do anything
But her response was silently to give him back her platinum ring

He did not mean it, his head was racing, just wanted some peace

Didn't realise how many times he hit her before he
felt some release

He never intended or expected it to go that way
But their lives were irretrievably ruined that bright
sunny day.

Because on that day, despite their love he caused
her death
And inadequate apologies to motherless children
was all he had left.

_____

A SIMPLE WOMAN'S PRAYER

Dear Lord, as I lay here all alone
I pray you help me find a decent man of my own.

They say beggars can't be choosers but as bad as
things may be
Please Lord, keep those brock pocket losers far
away from me

Like the type who says I am his, he doesn't need
another
Forgetting to mention he's still sleeping with three
of his five-baby mother

Or those who would say they love me to the
officers at
immigration
When all they love is a chance to be a citizen of
the British nation

I really couldn't stand one of them who get vex
and lay hands on me.
Because good God, no matter how sexy he may
be

Lord, you know me, I can't survive on prison food

But if he decide to lick me, believe I am going to get very rude

Lick for lick and tump for tump we'd have to fight all the way
And if I couldn't manage him, I might be forced to poison him one day

So, Lord, please look out for a nice brown skin man for me
And if he could have a little job, the happier I would be

If you give me the right man, my home and car we could share
Hold on…that last piece was said in a moment of despair

I believe my ideal man needs to have a car of his own
Because I really don't like the idea of a man just want to borrow and loan

But wait when I consider all the things involved in picking up a man
I believe washing my dirty skin and going to my bed alone is a much better plan.

Thank you, Lord,

Amen

SO, YOU BELIEVE YOU CAN HANDLE THIS? (X-RATED)

Me and my male friend were tight but nothing physical was going on
Knew him and his wife for years, our friendship was so strong

After a breakup I was feeling low, so he passed by for a chat
I thought why couldn't I find a caring brother like that?

Later as my boy was leaving, he suddenly tried to kiss me.
I thought he must be either drunk or charged surely

I told him that he must have bumped his head
If he thought I'd allow my friend's husband to get into my bed

He carried on so I warned him his heart may not stand the pace

I'm a serious woman, don't do my things like I'm running any race

He decided to ignore me and jumped up on my bed
I was so vex, had spent ages ironing that brand new spread

So, I got out my spray cream to add a little flavour to his parts
And some silk scarves to tie him down and blindfold his ass

He laid there in anticipation; I sprayed him with the cream
Boyfriend went crazy, this was a new experience it would seem.

I put the blindfold loosely over his eyes
He started begging me to hurry up with his surprise

I then said I just needed to make a call on my mobile phone
Man started boasting, asked if I couldn't handle it alone

I told him I didn't have a problem, I was just ringing his house
My man gasped then went silent, like a mouse

I said that if he decided he wanted to be with me
He would need to keep the whole damn night free

Didn't want his wife worrying he was dead on the
roadside
The fool believed me, even though you know I
lied.

He started thrashing about like he was possessed
I actually thought he might have a cardiac arrest.

Earlier he was whispering words of love and
affection
But now his obscenities to decent people, I
couldn't mention

Then he started begging, in-between the swearing
His voice was so high pitched I couldn't work out
what I was hearing.

He got up and ran around trying to cuss while
putting on his brief
His crusty looking bottom resembling an old piece
of tough beef

I wanted to suggest he needed a little Coco Butter
or Vaseline
But at the time the man was carrying on far too
obscene.

So, I thought it best to keep my opinion to myself
and said no more
Instead flinging his expensive jacket out of my
front door.

I warned him no matter how fast he drives to get
home
Even with a police escort I could reach first with my
phone

Asked him if he thought he would be met by his
loving wife's arms in bed
Or pure arms house and noise up in his head?

Out of my gate and down the road he ran
Couldn't believe for so many years I had adored
that man.

The moral of this is, you must not bite off more
than you can chew
Because if you push a decent woman to bite back,
she could finish you

MOVING ON

Have you ever felt mentally you were in a place
you did not belong?
Inside you just felt, something just feels wrong.

Emotionally you could be living in the City of
Doom
Those around you assassins to any happiness that
might bloom.

You can hear voices, not of the schizophrenic or
paranoid type
Trying to convince you that this is what your life
must be like

They tell you that men cheating on you is a way of
life
Friends will betray you with their tongues as
deadly as any knife.

And you're too stupid to be wanted as a partner or
a friend
And so, their mental attacks go on, without
reprieve or end.

We have all resided in the city of doom from time
to time
But you can give up your tenancy, I gave up mine.

I decided I had to get through the city's bolted
door
Ignoring the lies I had been told, picking my
self-esteem up off the floor

Remember our Creator specifically made me and
you
We are unique and precious, no one can do the
things we do.

First be kind to yourself, learn to care about your-
self a bit more each day
Finding something you like about yourself can turn
into
self-love along the way

Attending self-awareness seminars, reading
expensive motivational books is fine
But you need to create your own positive
thoughts, fix those in your mind

Seek those who appreciate you for who you are
and not what you can give.
You will eventually reach the City of Happiness,
where we all should aspire to live

Here others generate thoughts that are respectful
and kind
I call these thoughts the Guardian Angels of my
mind

There is Courage, Honesty and Confidence, to
name a few
They are a part of me, each helping me do the
things I need to do.

We all have these attributes; we'd readily use to
help a friend in need
Why not you, to ensure you live the life you
desperately need to lead

Believe me, I'm not perfect and all the answers I'll
never know
But each day I try to focus on making myself better
for tomorrow.

Some days it is so hard, but it's not always our
circumstances giving us pain.
It is our unwilling to learn, that keeps us going
back over and over again.

I have had to learn the common dominator in my
life's tragedies is me
So therefore, its only me who can decide how
different my life should be.

Having mentally arrived in the City of Happiness,
I'm working hard each day
Because I can finally, truly understand, it really is
the only way.

"BUT WHETHER WE FEEL IT COULD EVER BE POSSIBLE OR RIGHT IN ANYWAY,

TIME MOVES ON WITHOUT OUR CONSENT AND TOMORROW IS ANOTHER DAY."

WHERE I AM NOW, SURPRISED I STILL NEED TO CHECK MYSELF?

Section Three

LETTER FROM HOME

One day I received a letter from
someone saying she was a relative of mine
Well, not quite, but our families she swore, were
intertwined.

Said she heard I had a big job, good money
coming in
So, she was writing to request I sent her one or
two "little ting"

Wanted Marks & Spencer's clothes for her children,
I believe she has eight
Also, Clarks school shoes, and I should hurry as
she'd wrote her letter late.

Told me that I owed her as she'd changed my
nappies when I was a baby
That was a longstanding debt as at the time I was
a woman of fifty-three

Said things were hard, Jamaica was in recession, I
knew all about that
Had no job for six months now and was struggling
to even feed my cat

My "relative" said she needed to come to England
to "make life"
Wanted an invitation letter so she could find a rich
man and become his wife

Said she would need to come and stay at my
house or my flat
I thought before you tell me you're
staying; shouldn't you at least know that.

Said she's not begging; swore she'd repay the
money I was
giving her to get started
Reminded me of when granny used to say, "a fool
and his money are soon parted".

She demands with haste I must send the clothes,
shoes, and invitation letter
She has no time to waste, she's on a
mission to make her life better.

Said she can't understand why people living in
foreign were so mean
We just forgot our family at home, wouldn't even
send them a bean

Told me I should have a conscience and take some
responsibility
If our lives were turned around, she swears she'd
do the same for me.

Now, I didn't have a problem considering a
genuine family request
It's just I don't know who the hell she is and how
she find out my address.

—————————————

NONE SO BLIND AS THOSE WHO WON'T SEE

From an early age, I cannot lie, I always carried too
much weight.
Even though I complained sometimes,
mainly I just enjoyed what I ate.

But extra pounds never stopped me from making
the most of my time.
Had some pretty man and if my frock got
tight, I'd buy a bigger one, I was fine.

I'd encountered my fair share of fool, fool ashy
skinned guys.
Who thought they could handle me a way,
simply because of my ample size.

Forget that, my brain wouldn't allow me to be
anyone's damn clown
And with my machete sharp tongue, I had no
trouble chopping any of them down.

So early on I adopted a defiant attitude about my
unhealthy weight gain

Even when my body was so tired, a
little too sweaty or in real pain.

I refused to listen to the negative voices which
frequently shouted in my head
"Back away from the cake gal" or "leave that
extra slice of hard dough bread"

Told myself, as long as big sized clothes sold on
road or online
I worked hard, had good credit so those clothes
could always be mine

Now I wasn't oblivious, those health
threats did sometimes cross my mind
Even I could not ignore the thought that one
day soon I might not be fine.

So Weight Watchers and
Slimming World made thousands from me
Problem was, I'd lose two pounds and had to
reward myself with KFC

But one morning everything was a blur, like I'd
smeared Vaseline over my eyes
My optician shook his head and said "my dear,
this comes as no surprise"

He told me my eyes were the type that diabetes
would make blind
And despite his many years of warning, to my

body, I had never been kind.

Nothing could ever have prepared me for the
devastation I felt that day
The worst thing was, I had no excuses, I
had caused things to go that way.

I always prided myself on working hard and
having achieved so much.
But I couldn't work, care for my granny,
and drive my convertible only by touch

Foolishly I'd never prioritised giving my body
the care it needed to thrive
And then I was being told I had to depend on
medication to keep me alive

Real sickness and fear woke me up, only because I
was now in pain
And through fear, hard work and family support I
got my eyesight back again.

I know diabetes can attack those who've done
nothing wrong and are perfectly slim.
My own son in law cannot live without his
five times a day injection of insulin.

So, whilst I'll never be skinny, from too much sugar
I have learnt to stay.
Though this menopause madness is now
conspiring to force my waistline to stray

Those extra pandemic pounds have crept on
slowly, but boy I'm fighting back.
Because now I reach 60, I cannot afford for my
health to come under attack.

For years I lied to myself more than to others that I
didn't care about my weight.
Weird but I'm actually grateful diabetes
taught me self-care
before it was too late.

It's a daily battle but every time I wake up and I can
clearly see.
I know the battle's worth it, as the only
winners are my beautiful family and me.

SURELY THE PARENTS MUST SHARE THE BLAME

Something is going on outside, is that a police car
I can see at no. 34?
What is this neighbourhood coming to, never had
the police at my door?

I used to love living here with other hardworking,
decent folk
Now the neighbours are not "our type" although
we've never actually spoke

That one has several children but no partner as far
as I am aware
Although I have seen several different men visiting
there.

Doesn't work so heaven knows how she affords
fancy clothes for her boys
And her girls are always playing with expensive
toys

All I know is that we have worked hard to bring up
our only son
Paid for his private school, couldn't consider a
State one
We gave our boy all the advantages in life, kept

our family intact
Statistics say that this helps children stay
grounded, that is a fact.

Every day we're bombarded with horrific tales of
murder on the news
Politicians from every party being called on to
express their views

Knife and gun crime is now a daily topic on every
television station
Total fear and disbelief have gripped the entire
nation

It's disgraceful that people think so little of human
life
That they could attack another human being with a
gun or a knife

What kind of upbringing have they had, these
youths ruining the lives of others?
Their parents must know what's going on,
especially their mothers

Their responsibility to protect society from their
offspring is real
They should stop them from maiming others and
trying to steal.

I despair of the times we live in and am just
grateful we brought up our son right

He always tells me where he is going, day or night.

I am so afraid for innocent young men like my son
when they are out alone
I cannot consider going to sleep until he is safely
home.

My neighbours' primal screams bring me back to
reality
As I reach the door I see two officers, they're
asking to speak to me

One says something, everything is spinning, he
repeats what he said
"There has been an incident and the young man
across the road is dead"

But that is not the part that is making me physically
sick
He tells me that the murderer is my son, my
darling Patrick

I have to go now; they say my boy is distraught
and calling for his mum
As I leave people stand staring at me as if I was
some type of scum.

I keep repeating "we are decent, how could this
happen, I really did not know
Which parent can always be aware of what their
children do and where they go?"

YOU DID GET LOCKDOWN OR LOCK OFF?

When Boris seh man, woman and chile haffi
lockdown in a dem home,
Mi first reaction was "merciful Jesus, how the hell
mi a goh manage alone?"

My man use Friday night ludo with him friend as
cover to spend the night with me
When no more game nah play, how the hell him a
goh get free?

Mi noh know if 'im live wid 'im main squeeze or if
she ah him wife,
if she a work from home or even have a job – me
never want know bout people life

All dem phone call me use to get when my man
was on road (or by him friend)
now mi phone so silent, I coulda swear it bruk or
my contract come to an end.

No morning text, no likkle video, not even a phone
call from the toilet me cyaan get
Come on, you really mean to seh, about me, my
man nah fret?

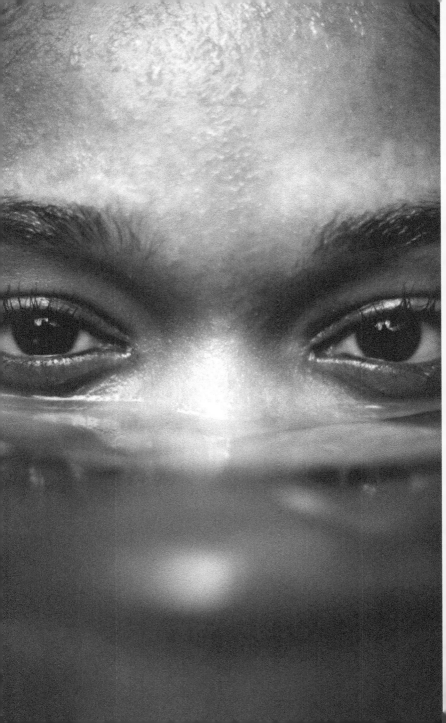

Me always seh me ah di clever one - have up odda
people property
I tek the best and leave the rest for the gyal a yard,
me is my man's no 1 priority.

Cause even if I cyaan cook, my man always
Deliveroo mi the best food
And him will drop everything to reach my yaad
when I tell 'im I want to get rude

Now dis government come ah tell people dat dem
must stop walk street
Even ah threaten me, not even mi madda and
fadda me cyaan meet

Now whole heap o' people pon road seh dere is
no Covid, mi cyaan seh eida way
But me hear seh nuff people get sick and dead soh
really
people noh want fi play.

But Covid mek mi a suffer now tru me used to de
man ah give me little change
Mi cyaan afford Waitrose or Sainsbury now, even
Iceland outta my range

Bwoy, mi remember ah Selfridges, River Island and
JD Sports we used to go
Boris mek the people lock them shop, like the man
from Delmonti, him said "No".

Mi cyaan believe a man seh him care 'bout you but
'im cyaan call in a year and a half
Is either 'im wrap up wid 'im wife or 'im an' a new
gyal ah sid down and a laugh

Even if 'im call me now and seh why 'im was under
serious pressure to stay away
Me noh too sure if mi want di badda - big ol'
woman lakka me, way too ol' fi play

Imagine mi hear seh him deh 'bout soh mi know
him noh dead but still no call
Mi pride ah tell me seh he must still want me, but
me brain seh him no care at all

My fren big mouth Felicia tell me dat fi har man
never once lef har out
She ah side chick but figet covid, wife and six
pickney- fi har man always deh 'bout

But to tell the truth me noh too sure 'bout Felicia
as she might ah tell me lie
Seh she have man fi six years now, but mi never
spot him one day yet with my eye

She same one tell me "it's col' out there, man
scarce, hold your corner til him reach"
But right now mi feel fi goh out and find him with
one bottle of bleach

Cause me cyaan tek shame, mi always run things, but now mi is asking yuh,
"If the man noh even deh yah legal, him ah listen to what Boris ah tell him fi duh?"

Down to Boris best friend dem de Cummins and de Hancock, nah duh wha him ah say
Bwoy, mi vex yuh know, feel like the whole breed o' man fi jus' goh weh

My best friend Claudette sensible, she seh me need fi check me owna behaviour
As wedda di man is alive or dead, good or bad, him is not mi saviour.

She seh instead of mi ah encourage people man fi lay down inna my bed
Mi shoulda spend mi time ah look 'bout putting sitten sensible inna mi head

She ask mi why at my big ole age, me still nah tek my life seriously
If me noh want good fi myself, how me expect a man fi want good for me?

Soh Boris, even doah mi cyaan stomach yuh and yuh liared fren' dem
You really show me, ah only me responsible fi sort out my business inna di end.

Because when things get serious people mek

choices and show who a dem priority
And if you get lock off, best believe, you was only
an option, just like me.

Find a way to set up yuhself right so nobaddy cy-
aan just tek your lifestyle away
Nutten come easy, but yuh can change up tings
when yuh decide today is the day.

THE REAL DEAL

I had tried to speak positively about this
menopause thing
Stated yes it would be difficult but as strong black
women we wouldn't let it win

But hear what, then the harsh reality of the
menopause took hold
And I wouldn't even try to pretend that I am
feeling big, bad and bold

No matter who you are as women our lives can
sometimes be tough
Worthless man, fastie pickney, money worries,
sisters we've all had it rough.

But you'd think that the one person you could
always depend on was you
Before this madness that's something I thought I
definitely knew

But now between forgetfulness and mood swings,
I'm doubting my own sanity
As a lawyer it's not a good thing to be wondering if
they're all fools or is it me?

I got people chatting to me a way, believing that
their acting reasonably
I'm thinking I could argue provocation when I kill
them and still getaway free

As a big girl I have always gone over and above to
keep myself so clean
Didn't ever want to be one of those unfortunates
who were smelt before their seen

Come on folks, we're big people, we're keeping
this thing real
Cause as decent as we are, we all know the deal

Whilst skinny girls can run around all day looking
good and hardly even perspire
I just have to think about running for a bus, to
break out a sweat and smell dire.

This blasted menopause has my years of hard work
going down the drain
Hot flushes got my body smelling like some old
dawg catch out in the rain.

But forget all that, today I have bigger problems to
focus on
Like many women of our age our partners had
decided it was time to move along

I can happily confirm that after spending time in

the wilderness alone
I got a decent black man who wants to regularly
frequent my home.

But this menopause is trying to mash up my
business with my man
Ladies you know when you've had a call and set up
a plan

You bathe, pick out your outfit and make yourself
look and smell just right
Ready for that special brother to come over and
make your night

Last Saturday night I must admit I don't even hear
my man come in
He said I was snoring so loud I even drowned out
Beres with my din.

Imagine being found dead to the world, lipstick
smeared across my face in bed
When all day I'd been planning X -rated, big
people business in my head

On top of that we've had a pandemic, government
ordered us all to stay at home
Do you know how much coronary inducing food
I've consumed alone?

It's the menopause's fault I can now only fit into
house clothes

This wouldn't have happened if Boris didn't force all the shops to close

Those who know me will definitely be able to confirm to any of you
That loving my family, working hard and shopping even harder is all I do

So being locked away from everything that defines me
Whilst growing a moustache and getting fatter isn't a good look for anybody.

Yesterday hot flushes were killing me, decided I needed some sweet cake to eat
Remaining naked to keep cool meant I weren't going on the street

So, I made an online order of something deliciously creamy and sweet
Planning to chill and watch a movie, resting my poor swollen feet

Being absent minded I nearly killed the Deliveroo man
It really was unfortunate and certainly wasn't my plan

You see, I forgot I was naked when I approached my glass front door today
I don't know who was more frightened as he

screamed loudly and ran away

By the time I grabbed a dressing gown and
opened my front door
There was no sign of him, just my mash up food
dash down on the floor

My lawyer instincts immediately thought to
complain, get the boy the sack
Then I thought, could you really stand to read the
comments they may write back.

I can't protect myself from the menopause but can
avoid more food over my floor
Oh, got to go the Amazon prime man is here with
the blinds for my front door.

SHE'S GONE

Vibrant, loving and kind women taken in their prime
However, they passed does not matter, simply gone before their time.

Significant women disappearing from our world but not from our hearts
No more will they quietly, honourably play their parts.

Our mothers, sisters, friends and colleagues each and every one
Our girls we would always rave with, cry with, simply have fun

Some knew their time was limited and tidied up their affairs
Preparing for when our tomorrow would not be theirs

Others were sudden and we are left with grief and shock
Their passing was like the stopping of every single clock

The tears, what ifs, how could this be?
All the while thinking "thank you Lord this time it
was not me"

But whether we feel it could ever be possible or
right in anyway
Time moves on without our consent and
tomorrow is another day.

These quality women wouldn't want us turned
into fossils by our pain
That should not be their legacy and this
behaviour simply brings no gain.

They must be honoured by those of us who
continue after they've gone
We must celebrate new experiences, taking their
memory along

A close friend told me she had an illness which
she couldn't fight
Felt it was a privilege to know, rather than crying
over her plight

Wanted to repair a relationship damaged by a
stupid fight
Take the opportunity to tell her family she knew
they would be alright

Would address issues she had with her mum and
we all have one or two

She did things she could not bear to pass without
having the time to do.

I admired how she accepted she was losing her
final battle in life
Whilst my pain at losing her felt as sharp as being
cut by a knife

She said I shouldn't worry as there is nothing I
could do
No one escaped life alive but passing was easier
by having friends like you

I recently visited a friend's family home where
someone had died
Beautiful cards and flowers on every surface near
and wide

I believed it was a beautiful thing
But hoped that those well-wishers had visited the
deceased or gave her a ring

My grandad, used to always tell me when I was a
child
At funerals you'll see some screaming and carrying
on wild

Their consciences may be troubling them as they
were not often there
When the deceased could have dearly benefited
from their care

So, a suitable tribute to honour our sisters who've
gone ahead to pave our way
Is to be a good friend whilst we are still here today

As we do not know what tomorrow brings to each
and every one
We need to live our lives to the full and make sure
we have real fun

Because all too soon our lives, like theirs will have
come and gone
And to have wasted that precious time would be
so very wrong.

"REMEMBER OUR CREATOR SPECIFICALLY MADE ME AND YOU

WE ARE UNIQUE AND PRECIOUS, NO ONE CAN DO THE THINGS WE DO."

THANK YOU FOR YOUR SUPPORT

www.justiceverseslife.com

Lightning Source UK Ltd.
Milton Keynes UK
UKHW020633060323
418094UK00011B/240